MY IMAGINATION STATION
ELIZABETH GOES TO SCHOOL

WRITTEN BY
TIFFANY PRINCE

ISBN: 978-1732487307

This book is dedicated to my beautiful daughters,
Madison & London. Always remember you are
POWERFUL.
Whatever you IMAGINE is already yours. Use your
MIND, or as we call it
IMAGINATION STATION,
and create your MAGIC!!!
I LOVE YOU ALWAYS!

Elizabeth sat crying on her bedroom floor, The Princess Palace, as her Mom rubbed her back.

She said "Today was a bad day Mommy, I didn't make any friends and no one wanted to play with me at school."

Elizabeth's Mom went to Elizabeth's toy chest and got seven of her favorite dolls. Elizabeth looked at her Mom strangely as she wiped a tear from her eye and said, "what are these?"

Her Mom answered in a gentle voice, "Play with your new friends just like you will at school tomorrow."

"Remember to give them names and introduce yourself! Let your new friends ask you to play and have fun. Make this playtime into the day you wished today would have been.

Oh and Elizabeth... remember to use your **IMAGINATION STATION** to make it real!"

"Elizabeth, wake up it's time to go to school" her Mom yelled. "But Mommy, I need one more minute…please" Elizabeth wined.

"Ok, if you promise to focus on what a great day you're going to have! The **IMAGINATION STATION** works best with **FOCUS!**" said her Mom.

Elizabeth yawned and went back to sleep as she thought about all the kids wanting to play with her.

When Elizabeth's Mom woke her up, she got ready for school quickly! On the way out the door she asked, "Mommy is it ok if I take one of my dolls with me today?" "Of course you can but your **IMAGINATION STATION** is more powerful than a doll can ever be! It's the feeling that you must hold onto, just as you hold onto your doll sweetheart."

Elizabeth went to school that day and it seemed as if something magical happened!

When she went to class one of the most popular girls saw Elizabeth's doll in her backpack.

For the rest of the day the popular girl not only talked to Elizabeth, she asked to play with her at recess! As recess approached, Elizabeth and her new friends played dolls and all the girls in her class joined in!

At that very moment Elizabeth realized this was exactly how she had played last night with her dolls in "The Princess Palace" She thought to herself, "Mom's right, I really do have **SUPER POWERS** and that is **MY IMAGINATION STATION!**

Elizabeth loved school and her new friends. She was now one of the most popular girls in her school! Everything was going great until a new student was transferred to her class. His name was Robert and he seemed to get a kick out of making fun of the girls.

The girls would tell the teacher but that didn't stop Robert. Once he saw how popular Elizabeth was he got jealous. He thought why does Elizabeth have all the fun and friends? The love Elizabeth got made Robert mad. He wanted to be loved too. If Robert only knew he had an **IMAGINATION STATION.**

21

Elizabeth's **IMAGINATION STATION** came into her mind but she wasn't sure how playing with dolls was going to make Robert leave her alone.

When she got home from school she ran to her dollhouse.

She put a boy and girl doll on the floor and yelled for her Mom. "Mom I need your help, the fake Robert is messing with all the girls at school and their scared!"

Elizabeth's Mom sat down and began to play. "Ok Elizabeth the first time we used your **IMAGINATION STATION** you focused on the love you felt

when you were playing with the girl dolls, right?! Yes Mommy, I did" said Elizabeth. "I want you to use that same focus. Your **IMAGINATION STATION** doesn't work without focus."

"Remember Elizabeth focus on **LOVE** and **LOVE** only. You see every time we play dolls and the boy doll Robert makes fun of you, you get sad. Elizabeth you have to stay **FOCUSED** no matter what. Focus on the love you know Robert has inside even if he is not showing it.

Think about how you want Robert to act instead of how he is acting and watch it unfold."

"Don't get upset if Robert does something he always does, just say, Robert I know your full of love you just don't know how to show it. Imagine him leaving you alone. You think you got it baby or do you want to keep playing **IMAGINATION STATION?**" "No I got it Mommy, I can't wait to see how Robert acts in school tomorrow!"

The next day Elizabeth went to school prepared to hold Robert's highest and best self in her mind no matter what!

She remembered her Mom saying without focus the **IMAGINATION STATION** doesn't work.

As Elizabeth reached her classroom all of her classmates ran to tell her Robert wasn't in their class anymore. The Principal found out Robert had been bullying a little girl in another class and removed him from the school. This was the first time Elizabeth's **IMAGINATION STATION** worked even better than she expected! She didn't have to do anything but show up to school.

When Elizabeth got home that day she thought to herself, what did I do different?

She played with the same dolls every time she used her **IMAGINATION STATION.** As she sat and thought hard, two things came to mind.

1. Elizabeth focused on **LOVE** only this time when she played **IMAGINATION STATION.**

2. Elizabeth also focused on Robert's best self no matter **WHAT!**

It seemed that these two things made Elizabeth's magic work better and faster!

Elizabeth made sure she would never forget that or her **IMAGINATION STATION!**

www.ingramcontent.com/pod-product-compliance
Lightning Source LLC
Chambersburg PA
CBHW041547040426
42447CB00002B/72

* 9 7 8 1 7 3 2 4 8 7 3 0 7 *